Advice for Insecure Writers

Charles Ray

Uhuru Press

North Potomac, MD

Charles Ray

Cover design and illustrations by the author.

Published in the United States of America.

ISBN: 0692526862
ISBN-13: 978-0692526866

DEDICATION

To all the people out there who would rather be writing than almost anything else, and to those who support and encourage them.

CONTENTS

Introduction

There's an old adage, "Everyone has at least one good book in them." Probably true—most likely true—but, if you're that person with that 'one good book,' I'm not talking to you. The only advice I have for you is; go ahead and write the damn thing and be happy.

If, though, you fancy yourself a *writer*, that is someone who has a lot of good books, a lot of not-so-good books, and maybe even a great book or two in you, well, pay attention, because you are the target of this book.

Writers are by nature solitary creatures. The solitude necessary to really write, though, can also breed a degree of insecurity. There's often no one we writers can turn to in order to relieve the feelings of inadequacy and fear that plague us all.

In my own case, I've been writing since my teens. I grew up in a small East Texas town where prowess in sports or shooting was considered the only proper thing for manly men, and unless you planned to become a teacher or preacher (or, if you had the connections and stomach for it, an undertaker) you were expected to be a farmer or lumber worker. I was, therefore, a pretty lonely kid, spending most of my time alone, reading or writing silly stories that I made up. As you might imagine, I took a lot of teasing from my peers, and got a lot of sympathetic looks from adults—not very good at instilling confidence, let me tell you.

I got a little relief when I enlisted in the army after high school. I can just imagine people in my home town thinking that the army would finally turn me into a real man. I actually quit writing for a while—for a whole year—but, only because that first year in the army involved some pretty intensive training, leaving no free time to write.

When I was assigned to Germany, though, with a more predictable work schedule, the notebooks came out again. I was regularly published in the 'Pup Tent Poets' section of the European edition of *Stars and Stripes*. I never shared any of this with my family or friends back home. They wouldn't have understood. And, get this, even though I was being published, I still harbored doubts about my ability as a writer.

Over the next 20+ years, I was regularly published in newspapers and magazines, in the U.S., Europe, and Asia, got poems published in a few anthologies, and I still had doubts about my ability. I wanted to write books, but I was scared. I had, somehow, convinced

myself that I couldn't do it.

I was the classic insecure writer.

After I retired from the army, I joined the U.S. Foreign Service, and served as a diplomat in posts in Asia and Africa, and the amount of official writing I had to do in these jobs kept me from what I really wanted to do—write creatively. Or, so I led myself to believe.

Then, during one of my rare U.S. assignments as an American diplomat, someone (I no longer remember who) mentioned that my ability to find the best turn of phrase, to write official memos that people enjoyed reading, ought to be shared outside government. Someone who was not a writer or editor was actually telling me that I could write.

Well, I knew that all along. Whenever I had to write an official document, I mentally went through the same process any writer, fiction or nonfiction, goes through, the same process I'd used during the 60s and 70s when writing newspaper and magazine articles. And, editors back then had thought what I wrote worthy enough to actually pay me for it.

That's when I realized that it hadn't been the criticisms or lack of approval from others that had been holding me back. It had been *me* and my irrational fears, my insecurity. I had convinced myself that I wasn't a *real* writer.

At that moment, I decided that I would write something longer than a magazine article. I would write a *book*. No, not a book, but a lot of books. I had all these ideas that had been nibbling at the edge of my consciousness for years. Now I would turn them into reality.

Making that decision was the first step. That was the hardest because it had taken me so long to do it. The next steps were also hard, and took a long time, but they weren't crippling. They were just hard work. The first nonfiction book, *Things I Learned from My Grandmother About Leadership and Life*, took three years to write. My first full-length work of fiction, *Color Me Dead*, which I actually started before the nonfiction book, took much longer—over seven years, in fact. But, despite setbacks, and more rewrites than I can count, I persevered. That book, the first in my Al Pennyback mystery series, was 19 books ago for the series, and nearly 60 overall.

I didn't analyze the process I went through at first. I was too happy, and too busy, just writing. But, when I came across a UK-based blog, Alec Cavanaugh's 'Insecure Writer Support Group,' I began to think about what had made me fearful and insecure. I joined the group of bloggers who contribute advice and experiences on the first Wednesday of each month, I began to write about the things that had bothered me, and in so doing, I came to the conclusion that I'd quite accidentally conquered my own insecurity. I might not be a best-seller, but I AM a writer, and I will no longer let myself convince myself that I'm not.

If you've had these bouts of insecurity, times when you sit and stare at the screen, and nothing seems to happen, I'm hoping the bits of advice I offer here will help you to discover the same thing I did. That, you are the one who decides that you're a writer, and once you've made that discovery and developed the confidence to put what you write before the reading public, with practice and perseverance, you can become a successful writer. How you define that success is also up to you, and it's not the subject of this book—maybe another time.

I hope you'll find a useful nugget or two within these pages; a bit of advice that breaks the logjam that's clogging up your creative conduits, and frees your creative juices to flow freely. If you do, I'd really appreciate hearing from you. You can contact me at charlesray.author@yahoo.com. And, if you like what you've read, I would also appreciate a review, even a few words, on Amazon, Goodreads, or any other book review site. After all, we writers write in order to be read, and reviews attract readers.

Happy reading.

How do You Know You're a Writer?

Webster's New Universal Unabridged Dictionary gives the following definitions for **writer:**

writ'er, n. 1. one who writes, has written, or is in the habit of writing.

2. a person whose business or occupation is writing; specifically, (a) a copyist; a scribe or clerk; (b) an author, journalist, or the like.

This book is for those who fall under definition 2(b). Just what is an author, and how do you know if you are one? Well, if you've written and published a book, whether or not it's sold more than the obligatory number of copies to your family and friends, I'd say you qualify, wouldn't you?

Actually, though, I think there's even more to it than Mr. Webster's tome implies. I personally think that if you find yourself imagining stories when you should be doing something else, making notes about things you see and hear; then you, my friend, are a writer. You might be yet be unpublished, but if you would rather be writing than watching TV, you're probably a writer. If you write more than a letter home asking your folks for money, you're a writer. Got it?

The First Time I Knew I Had to be a Writer

This is a post I wrote for one of my blogs; *Free flow of ideas is the cornerstone of democracy,* on February 17, 2012.

I've been writing for as long as I can remember. Until my freshman year in high school, I was painfully shy and ill at ease around people, so I sought refuge in books. My mother taught me to read when I was four, and I went through the first and second grade readers at my school during the first month. Perplexed, my teacher let me sit by myself and read books from the school library's meager collection while the other kids struggled with 'See Spot run.' By the end of third grade, I'd made my way through the entire library, including the works of Edgar Rice Burroughs and Shakespeare. The archaic language of the Bard's works threw me at first, but when I figured it out, the language sang to me.

Throughout my school years, I spent time reading and making up stories about mythical worlds and nonexistent people. At the age of twelve or thirteen – after over fifty years it's hard to recall – I won a national Sunday school magazine short story competition. Seeing my name in print hooked me on 'seeing my name in print,' but it didn't make me know that I wanted to be a 'writer.'

When I turned 17, I joined the army, and six months before my 18th birthday found myself stationed in southern Germany. I loved reading the *Stars and Stripes*, especially the "Pup Tent Poets" section, so I started creating poems and submitting them. I had almost a one hundred percent acceptance rate, and again I was thrilled by the heady feeling of seeing my name in print, but still didn't think of myself as a writer. I was just someone who liked to write.

Over the next twenty years, I wrote frequently; contributing travel and historical articles to regional, national, and international publications, and even moonlighting as a free lance newspaper reporter in a few places. Along with the writing, I also did cartoons and other pictures, and photography for a number of publications and organizations. I loved doing it, and even made a little money from it, and, of course, still got a kick out of seeing my byline in a publication. But, I still didn't think of myself as a 'writer,' 'artist,' or 'photographer.' It was just something I did in my spare time because I loved doing it. Considering myself a writer would have been a professional, and life-changing decision, so I was perfectly content to leave things the way they were.

Then, I got smacked in the kisser with a lollapalooza of an epiphany, when, at the urging of a colleague, I wrote a little book on my leadership philosophy, "Things I Learned from my Grandmother About Leadership and Life," which was published in 2008. It wasn't, and isn't, a best seller, but a few people actually bought it and read it, and one of those people sent me an e-mail that changed my perspective significantly. She said that reading my book had changed her life; seeing what I'd learned as a child from my grandmother, and how I'd applied that knowledge throughout my life, gave her a better sense of herself and a new lease on life. She then went on to say that she'd given the book to her teenage son to read, and it made an immediate change in his behavior, and caused him to turn his life around, from the self-destructive path he had been on.

As I read her email, I thought to myself, "So, this is what writers can do. Maybe, this is what I've been working toward all these years." See, writing and being a writer are two vastly different things. When you write because you love to write, or even because you're compelled to write, it can be an exercise to just please yourself. But, when you consider yourself a writer, you than have to consider others – the readers who will be educated, amused, or inspired by what you write. It's no longer just you sitting down with pen and pad, or keyboard, and spewing your thoughts onto the page. You have to develop a professional attitude about it; learn the mechanical techniques, read with a more critical eye to learn better ways of expressing thoughts, consider the impact your words will have on someone else. It's the difference between being a weekend golfer tearing up the landscape for fun, or an aspiring golfer who wants to get a card for the professional tour. You have to focus. After finishing that email, my mind was made up. Not only did I like to write, but I knew that I wanted to be a writer. That meant that I'd have to do much more than just sit down and scribble my musings into a journal every day – something I'd been doing for over 40 years, but I'd have to do it with purpose. I would have to work harder at polishing my writing; learning more about effective use of dialogue, character development, plot arc, and the like.

I no longer merely 'had' to write; I knew that day that I 'had to be a writer.'

Writer's Block and Other Barriers to Writing

Every writer at some point suffers the dreaded affliction known as writer's block—that situation when you stare at the blank paper or screen, and nothing, absolutely nothing comes to mind.

No one's really sure what causes this condition, but after looking back over my own experience, I have a few idea—well, one good idea, actually. Writer's block is caused by fear.

That's right: fear, or to put it another way, F.E.A.R., which is an initialism I encountered some time ago that stands for **F**orget **E**verything **A**nd **R**un. Sort of the feeling you get when the words just won't flow. But, what can cause this kind of unreasonable, irrational panic? I think it's a complicated combination of fear of failure, fear of rejection, and fear of success. The first two are probably easy to understand, but the third needs some explanation.

Let's say you've written a book, published it, and it did relatively well. Got a few good reviews, and is selling well. Now, people are anxiously awaiting your next. And, it scares the hell out of you. Can you live up to the expectations? The result of this kind of thinking is brain freeze. Believe me, I know it—I've been there.

There are ways, however, to deal with these kinds of situations. Ways that have worked for me, and that I'm sure will work for anyone.

Set Yourself a Daily Writing Quota

Way back in the dark ages of the 1970s I moonlighted as a newspaper journalist, alongside my day job as the assistant public affairs officer of an army base where I was stationed—a job in which I was in effect the managing editor of the base newspaper. In both jobs, I had to deal with crusty old southern newspaper editors who had cut their teeth as reporters in the 50s and 60s. One of them, and I no longer remember which, told me that the best way to improve my writing skills was to write a certain amount every day. It didn't matter, he said, how much, or about what, as long as you wrote *something*. He suggested 1,000 words a day, which was reasonable in the age of manual typewriters and ballpoint pens.

I've always been something of an over-achiever, though, and I also learned touch typing in high school, so I decided, if 1,000 words a day was the standard for these old hunt-and-peck typists, I could do 2,000. It was hard for the first few weeks, but I soon discovered that if I followed the advice to write about *anything* that came to mind, it wasn't hard at all to write 2,000 words a day. In fact, when I'm in the midst of writing a novel, I find myself doing 5 to 6,000 words. If the muse is really kicking my butt, I've even done 10,000, although I don't recommend chaining yourself to your computer for the time it takes to do that (I'll explain that in the following article).

Stop Writing: Get Some Exercise

The following is a post I wrote on my blog, *Charles Ray's Ramblings*, on August 5, 2015, for Alec Cavanaugh's *Insecure Writer Support Group*, minus the introductory paragraph inviting readers to sign up for the group. If you're interested, the link will be given at the end of this book.

This month, I'm going to depart from the usual advice to writers, to wit, WRITE, WRITE, WRITE, and tell you that sometimes the best thing you can do for your writing is to STOP!

Given that I'm usually spouting off that the only way to write well is to write often, and my frequent suggestion of having a 1 – 2,000 word per day writing goal, my regular readers are probably scratching their heads in wonder right now. Bear with me, though, and you'll see the method to my madness.

Everyone has, no doubt, heard or read the old adage, 'a healthy mind makes a healthy body,' or something along those lines. The meaning of that is usually, a good mental attitude is important to maintaining physical health. But, scientific studies have shown that the opposite is also true: maintaining good physical health helps to improve brain functioning. Staying physically active, keeping your heart, lungs, and blood vessels healthy helps ensure adequate oxygen gets to all parts of the body, including brain cells. And, while we're talking about exercise, which is great for maintaining the physical plant—muscles, bones, vital organs—it's also great for conditioning the brain. That's right. Science has discovered that the brain has more plasticity than previously thought, and even in adulthood, can be improved through exercises such as puzzles, learning a new language, or learning to play a musical instrument.

Ideas, and the manipulation of language are a writer's stock and trade, which means that for us as writers, the brain is one of our most important possessions. It stands to reason, then, that we should keep it in top condition. So, to keep that idea engine humming along like a Mercedes Benz S500, step away from the computer for a short period every day. Get out and walk through the park—briskly. Start every other morning with a nice, heart pumping workout, or work the daily crossword—with a ballpoint pen.

You don't have to sacrifice any of your writing goals to do this. Like writing, exercise can be worked into a 24-hour day if you really want to do it. Turn off the TV for thirty minutes. You've seen that episode of *Buffy the Vampire Slayer* anyway. Get out and walk around the block

Your writing will be better for it.

Reading—the Next Best Thing to Writing

All good writers are also avid readers. As a means to learning the writing craft, reading is the next best thing to writing.

One source of anxiety for writers, which causes a feeling of insecurity, is the feeling that you know what you want to write about, but you can't think of the right words, or (*shudder, shudder*), you can't think of a thing to write about. This can happen to anyone, at any stage in a writing career.

By 1982, when I retired from the U.S. Army and joined the U.S. Foreign Service, I'd already been writing and published for 20 years. But, when I got to my first diplomatic assignment in China, and learned that one of my duties would include writing reporting and analysis cables (one of a diplomat's primary functions), I froze. I mean, I did the complete deer-in-headlights thing. Even when given a subject to write about, I found myself staring at a blank sheet of paper, without a clue how to begin (back in those days, we used IBM Selectric typewriters instead of computers). Fortunately, my army training had taught me the value of reconnaissance. Before going into battle, you study your enemy and the terrain. So, I pulled out copies of previous reports written at my organization, and studied them carefully. When I had a feeling for the way they were written, I went back to my typewriter and banged out my first one. It had to go through a few rewrites before my boss, the consul general, finally accepted it, but when he did, he congratulated me on a well-written despatch—the archaic word for reporting cables at the time.

You can see from that experience that this time of insecurity can strike anyone at any time. One way to prevent—or mitigate—it is to do what I did; read.

Read widely, but, especially read widely in the genre(s) that you want to write. Read the authors you like. See how they deal with things like character development, voice, narrative description, etc. Make a note of things that really impress you. This is not to suggest that you *copy* these things. Instead, try to achieve the same effect in your own writing, in your own words.

In addition to reading to see how other writers do it,

another way to get control of your insecurity is to read how-to books. There are thousands of them in print, some pretty good, and some pretty awful—or, maybe useless is a better word. But, you can learn something even from the so-so writing guides. If nothing else, they will give you some ideas that you can use when you sit down to write. At the end of this book I've included a list of some of the writing guides I've found particularly useful.

Music Appeases the Muse

Some people need absolute quiet in order to write; others need some background noise. I'm one of the latter. My favorite background noise happens to be music—and, thankfully, the Internet has a lot to choose from. I like to have Oldies from the 50s and 60s playing softly when I write, especially some of the old doo-wop melodies.

Maybe classical music is your thing. I can do that too, provided it's not piano music, which tends to grate on my nerves after two or three songs.

Sometimes, listening to music while you're doing research or outlining your writing project, can be just the thing to relax you and get rid of those nervous jitters that freeze your thought processes.

Of course, if you're the type who needs quiet, have at it. Unless you live in the deep countryside and have a room with good soundproofing, it'll be hard to achieve perfect quiet, but if that's what it takes to get the creative juices flowing . . . go for it!

Dealing with Criticism and Negative Reviews

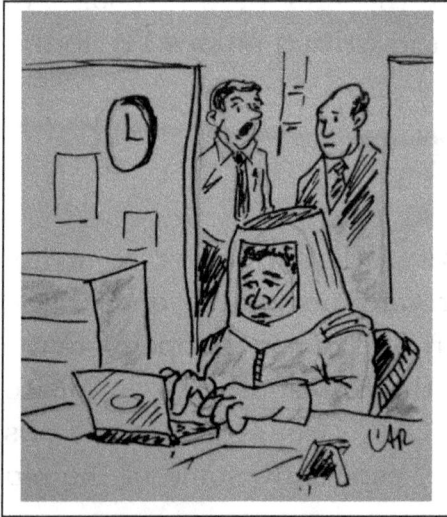

If you write for publication, one thing you cannot escape, and that can heap tons of insecurity upon your head, is the negative review. Along with that, there is the criticism from family and friends, sometimes well-meant, but often hurtful; who think you should really find something a little more *adult* to occupy your *free* time. While negative criticism can be debilitating, positive reviews, believe it or not, can also cause feelings of insecurity. In the first moments after reading a glowingly positive review, your head swells, and you're convinced that you're the next Hemingway. But, then, reality sets in, and you're seized with the thought—will I be able to live up to this in my next work? Was this first work just a fluke? It doesn't matter that your next work might be your second or your twenty-second— that dread that you can't *do it again* is always lurking in the background.

Let's get the positive reviews out of the way first.

They're great, but don't let them go to your head. Approach your next writing project as if it was the very first, and do your best to please your audience. Besides, that rave review just might have been your Aunt Nellie, who always praises what you do, so it really doesn't count.

Now, for those negative reviews or critiques' don't let them get you down. No matter how well you write, there will *always* be someone who won't like it. I once got a one-star review from a reader whose only complaint was that she disagreed with the way I used semi-colons. This type of review you can easily disregard. The reviewer who tears into you, though; who picks at every chapter, the characters, the plot, who just doesn't like what you wrote, that is a hard pill to swallow. But, you must. Because, if you don't you might find it hard—if not impossible—to write ever again.

One more important piece of advice. While it's okay to send a thank-you note to a reviewer who wrote nice things about your work, especially if you requested the review, or it's someone you know, don't ever engage the negative reviewer. That, believe me, is a no-win situation for either of you. Just move on. So, you know one person who doesn't like your writing. So what! There are millions of potential readers out there. Save your energy and effort for them.

Finally, here's a post I did on September 9, 2014, for Alec Cavanaugh's Insecure Writers Support Group on 'Dealing With Mindlessly Negative Reviews.'

My post this month is on dealing with not just negative reviews, but those that are mindless, pointless, vapid outpourings of people who probably haven't even read your book. If you publish what you write, you put your work out there for all to see – and comment upon. We all would like to get all five-star reviews that wax eloquent about our deathless prose and fantastic story-telling ability. But, not everyone will like what you write, so you have to be prepared for the occasional negative review. If you're smart, you'll not respond to such reviews, but you *will* take note of them, for they might just give you advice that could improve your future efforts.

There's one category of review, though, that is negative, and doesn't help you at all. That's the review that mindlessly slams your writing – often for the most vapid of reasons. The ease of posting comments (including reviews) on the Internet makes this one of the unavoidable facets of the writing life. How do you deal with it?

How, for instance, do you deal with a one-sentence, one-star review that doesn't even talk about your book? I recently received one of those, and after I stopped fuming, I laughed. The review said nothing about my book, so I don't know if the reviewer even read it. It was, however, a verified purchase, so, unless this person returns it for a refund, I at least get paid for it. As useless as it was, it also put the title out there for others to notice, and I can only hope that more rational readers will see the review for what it is – or isn't – and maybe be curious enough to get the book for themselves and form their own opinions.

In the meantime, I'll just keep on writing; keep putting my stuff out there; and hope for the best. Or, if not the best, at least more fair and legitimate reviews that help guide other readers to my work. Have any readers who are also writers received reviews that make no sense?

Charles Ray

Time to Get Serious

Now that you've done a few things to put your insecurity behind you, it's time to think seriously about your writing. In these next pages, I'll share with you some of the things I've learned over the years, and I hope you'll find them useful. Some I kind of learned by trial and error, others I picked up from others and played around with them until they fit my writing style, so I'm suggesting you do the same.

One of the first things you'll probably do is fritter around trying to decide which genre(s) you want to write in. You'll no doubt have been sharp enough to notice the way I wrote the word. If you're thinking that's because I think you should start by ignoring the well-meaning advice many writing books and authors give about writing in only one genre. Do you read only one genre? In that case, maybe you *should* only write in one genre, but how many people *read* only one genre? If you like reading a certain kind of story, you just might find that you can write that kind of story as well. Doesn't that make sense?

In the following articles I'll share some advice on writing for different genres, based on my own experiences. Some of these pieces are written especially for this book, and others are blog posts I've written over the past few years. Keep in mind as you read them that these are my experiences. What works for me might not be precisely right for you. But, they might just point you in a direction that *is* the right one for you.

What Does it Mean to Write What You Know?

I wrote this piece on March 4, 2015 for the *Insecure Writer's Support Group*. While it doesn't address the subject of genres specifically, it does address another old piece of writing advice: write what you know. No one has ever defined that piece of advice to my satisfaction, so I decided to speak my mind about it.

I want to talk this month about an issue that I've addressed before, but taking a different tack. If you've read any writing advice or instruction books, you're sure to have seen the commandment, 'write what you know.' Unfortunately, too many people take this advice quite literally, and believe they can only write about things they've personally experienced. Big mistake – and just plain wrong. Thing about it. If all writers took this advice literally, we'd have no great works of historical fiction. Think, for instance of Jean Auel's *Clan of the Cave Bear*. Since she wrote of prehistoric times, there's no way she could have

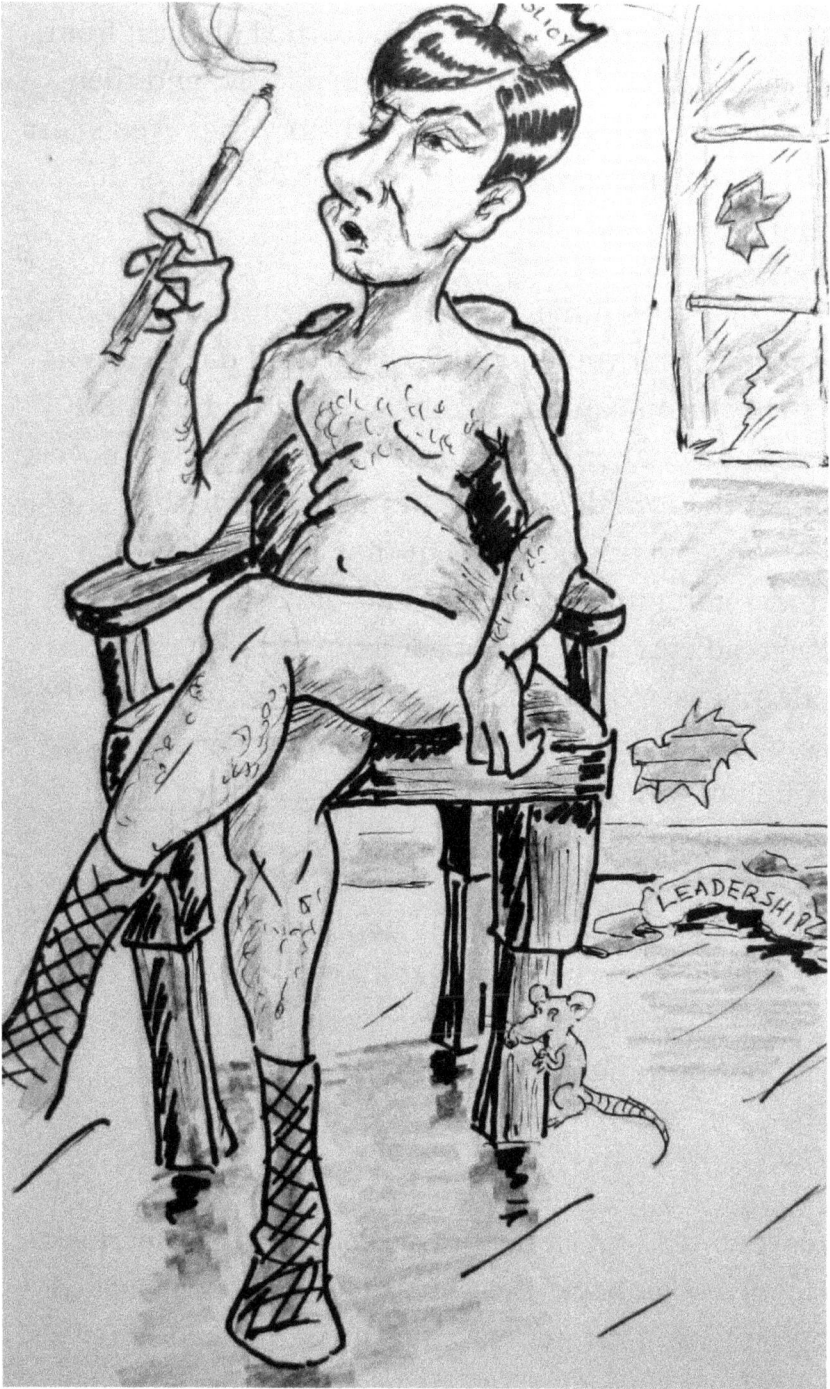

directly experienced it, or even learned about if from direct sources. She studied it intensively, and then used her imagination to create a story that even years later I remember vividly. Her book was even better than the movie.

So, what does it mean, 'write what you know'? I think it means that you should do what Auel did. Learn as much as you can about your subject, and then let your imagination do the rest. I write a series of novels about the Buffalo Soldiers of the post-Civil War era on the Western frontier. I spent time in the army, so I understand military tactics and protocol, but mainly I've read everything I can get my hands on about the era, the weapons, events, etc. And, I try to infuse the color of the time into my stories, all of which are fictional, with a backdrop of historical events for authenticity.

Unless you possess a completely blank brain, you can do the same. Write what you know, but resolve to know something new every day. That way, you'll never run out of things to write about.

How to Write Mystery Stories

I love to read mysteries. Ever since I read a Sherlock Holmes book back in grade school, I've been hooked on all type of mysteries, from the hardboiled PI novels to cozy mysteries. It was natural, therefore, that my first effort at writing book-length fiction would be in that genre. There are a number of great books on how to write mysteries. Following is the method I use.

I began my foray into mysteries with a story about a private investigator based in Washington, DC. Most of the mystery novels I've read—actually, most of the contemporary fiction—that have the nation's capital as a locale focus on politicians, spies, and high-powered lobbyists. I decided to take a different approach, so my focus would be on the everyday people who live in the city, which is one of the most diverse cities in the U.S.

Over the years, I've read a number of how-to books on the craft of the mystery, many useful, some not so much, but I've learned a lot from all of them. I've learned the most, though, just from the process of slaving over manuscript after manuscript, trying to make each story better than the one before.

I'd like to share some of the things I've learned through this process of trial and error in hopes that your journey will be easier than mine.

Let's start with the different category of mystery stories. In my own humble opinion, there are four main categories of the mystery story; the Puzzle Mystery, the Hard-boiled Mystery, the Pursuit Mystery, and the Straight Mystery.

The Puzzle Mystery: In the vein of Agatha Christie's *Miss Marple*, this category starts with a dilemma that the protagonist has to solve. While some books on the subject list Whodunits as a separate category, like the books written by Jack Higgins, these are, in my view, just puzzle mysteries with more technical stuff or procedural details.

Hard Boiled Mystery: Fans of Mickey Spillane will recognize these. They usually feature a lone PI who works the underbelly of the city, swamps, or Indian reservation. These stories are short on technical and procedural, but long on action. Very popular in the 40s and 50s, they have been partially replaced with stories of people working within or against organizations. My own mysteries, featuring a PI who sometimes works with, sometimes against, the system, fall somewhere between puzzle and hard boiled, with a touch of whodunit.

Pursuit Mystery: In this category the protagonist is on some important, often essential-to-survival quest. Eric Ambler is, in my opinion, a master of the pursuit mystery.

Straight Mystery: This is a bit of a cop-out on my part, but I use it to describe the kind of book that has a mystery as its main theme, but that is written as more or less straight fiction. John LeCarre and Georges

Simenon wrote great mysteries that weren't really mysteries.

What I like about the mystery genre is that it requires a certain structure. If you want to appeal to mystery fans you'd do well to know that structure well, and stray from it with extreme caution. That, though, is not why I like the mystery structure. As I'm not given to making detailed outlines before I start writing, beyond a basic theme, character lists, timelines, and the few technical details I plan to use in the story, knowing the structure helps to keep me focused. I start my mysteries with a general idea of how I want the story to end, and then I go back to the beginning and write until I get to where I want to be.

Despite not doing a detailed outline, I do stick to the basic anatomy of a good mystery story, keeping in mind that a writer should be first and foremost, an entertainer. If you stray from the basic structure, readers might feel a little uncomfortable, but if you entertain them they're likely to stick it out to see where you're going.

A mystery needs what any good story needs: a beginning, a middle, and an end. This three-act structure has been used effectively for ages, and is still the most effective way to maintain reader interest.

In addition to this basic structure, mystery stories need the following elements:

A Crime: It doesn't have to be murder, although most mysteries have at least one dead body. But, it has to be something a reader can identify with and care about, and it should be introduced very early in the story, preferably at the beginning. In one of my early Al Pennyback mysteries, *If I Should Die Before I Wake,* the crime was assault, but because it involved a woman in a coma who was introduced on the first page, readers were given something they could care about.

A Criminal: The perpetrator, or perpetrators, of the crime should be introduced early as well. In *Deadline,* two of the criminals were clearly identified early in the story, but the ring leader wasn't identified until the last few chapters. This character, though, was introduced early in the story, complete with clues, but also with a few red herrings to keep readers guessing.

Clues: In order to be fair and keep faith with your readers, clues to the solution should be presented, and as early as possible. This doesn't mean you shouldn't stick in a few false clues, but if you do, make sure you account for them at some point. The one thing you should never do is have the protagonist come up with a solution out of thin air. While it's okay to have your hero stumble around in the dark for most of the story, the solution *must* be supported by clues that, if the hero had access to them, so must your reader.

Conflict: Actually, conflict is important in any genre. Having barriers in your hero's way is a good way to keep the suspense level—and reader interest—high. The hero must continually be trying to catch the criminal, while the criminal is doing everything possible to avoid being caught. I think of conflict like this: In the beginning, put your hero up a tree. In the middle, throw rocks at him. To raise the level of conflict, throw bigger rocks. Then, in the end, let him come down.

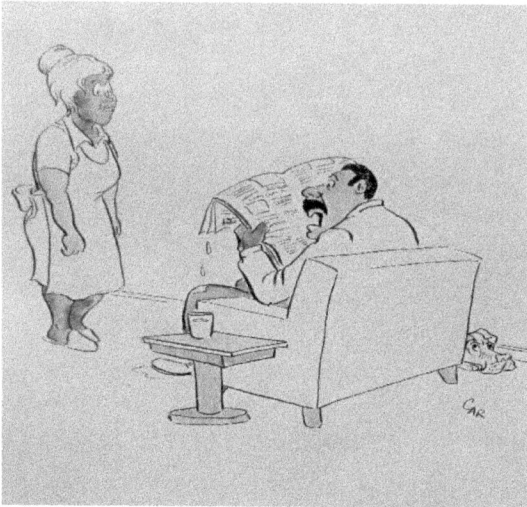

There's really no mystery to writing a mystery. All you have to do is keep these simple hints in mind. It's up to you how you apply them; outline or write by the seat of your pants, pick the subgenre you like—or even mix them up; but, if you keep the basic structure and essential elements in mind, you'll have a good story. Oh, and one other thing; while you're writing, have fun.

Writing Historical Fiction

My second series, but currently the most popular with readers, is about the Buffalo Soldiers of the Ninth U.S. Cavalry on the western frontier after the Civil War. While most of the readers are fans of Westerns, and think of them that way, my intent when I began the series was to do historical fiction—fictionalized accounts of the exploits of these valiant soldiers that are historically accurate.

For that reason, the hints that follow are about writing historical fiction. This article was published on *Charles Ray's Ramblings,* on November 6, 2013.

Writing historical fiction, while it does require a certain amount of research, is no more difficult than any other fiction. These helpful hints will get you started on your historical novel.

If you're a beginning writer without a clear idea of what genre to write in, you might want to consider historical fiction.

Now, if you're like most folks, you probably didn't pay too much attention during history classes in school – bored by all those dates and places – so, you're probably thinking historical fiction is not something you'd find easy to do. After all, it would mean doing research, and you hated doing that in school.

Think again. The historical fiction genre is currently ripe for picking, and the research you need to do to write it well can be fun. Why do I say it's ripe? Take a look at what's currently popular on TV and in the movies; historical films, some authentic, and some complete fiction. People are interested in the past as long as it's presented in an entertaining, easily digestible form.

Some Parting Shots on Genres

In addition to the two aforementioned genres, I've also written nonfiction, children's books, urban fantasy and a couple of books that really don't fit any neat categorization. With the exception of the nonfiction, I've found the three-act structure to be effective, and tend to use it. The elements to be included in a story differ from genre to genre, but it's pretty easy to look them up on line. As you become comfortable, though, you might want to experiment.

I wrote an urban fantasy that was also a parody of *Alice in Wonderland*, where I probably broke all the rules. In my book, *Wallace in Underland*, which was aimed at a young audience, I sought to entertain readers, but have subtle message against bullying and maltreatment of animals included as well. In the book, a young boy, Wallace Johnson, is alienated from his father and picked on by neighborhood bullies. Trying to escape the bullied one day, he encounters a talking rat, Ralph, who takes him to a mystical place underneath the city where he meets talking animals, many of whom have been victims of human abuse topside. I used a lot of puns and plays on words, and generally had a good time putting my strange cast of characters through their paces. In the end, Wallace grew and learned to deal with the problems in his life—it's always good to show your character growing out of his or her experiences—and, in the process, he saved the denizens of Underland.

Like I said, my aims with the book were to tell a fun story, and put across a message without sounding preachy. Virginia Phiri, a Zimbabwean author who is a good friend of mine, read *Wallace in Underland* at a school she visited a few years ago, and told me later that the kids really enjoyed the book, but also got the messages about the evils of bullying and mistreating animals. To me, that means more than making a best-seller list. But, I digress. What I hope has come across in this section of the book is that, conventional wisdom aside, you don't have to chain yourself to a single genre. Writing is hard work, but there's no law that says hard work can't also be fun. So, as you write, have a little fun.

Okay, You've Banished Your Insecurity, and You're Ready to Write Your Book—Now What?

The title of this section is probably overly optimistic. You never *completely* get rid of insecurities. What you do is get them under control to keep them from immobilizing you and taking over your life. But, that wouldn't have made a good title for a section, would it?

Okay, now that you're no longer burdened with that truckload of insecurity, let's get started writing. What, you have no idea what to write? Where do you get ideas, you ask? Well, I'm glad you asked. The following two articles, which appeared on *Charles Ray's Ramblings* talk about that very subject.

Where Ideas Come From – Part 1

This one ran on April 1, 2015

Ideas for writing come from all kinds of places.
My *Buffalo Soldier* historical series grew out of a
combination of inspirations. One day, I was sitting at

my computer, surfing the Internet, and I came across a site about the Buffalo Soldiers of the 9th and 10th US Cavalry on the western frontier, and I realized that not many Americans know a lot about the colorful history of these African-American soldiers and the role they played in the westward expansion of the country.

The germ of an idea was planted. What if I did a series of short stories (more like novelettes actually) that introduced them to readers? The more I thought about it the more it excited me. Several years ago, when I lived in North Carolina, I was a writer and artist for a short-lived magazine, *Buffalo* that was based in California. I had a regular cartoon feature, did a few historical articles, and did the illustrations for several of the magazine's covers.

So, I already had a bit of grounding in the subject; it was just a matter of how to kick it off. I decided to center it on a few fictional characters, with the main character, Sergeant Benjamin Franklin Carter, and show the kinds of activities they were engaged in. While I strive to make it historically accurate, I try to avoid long lectures on history. Instead, I insert the historical facts and incidents in through the characters' dialogue, or short descriptive passages to establish context. My main objective is to tell an interesting story that will keep the reader turning the page.

I can't be sure I've succeeded. Reader feedback has been limited, but what has been received is encouraging. raise indeed. My friend, Zimbabwean author Virginia Phiri (*Highway Queen*), who has read and reviewed a number of my books, also commended the series, describing them as 'good writing, and good reading.'

I use a lot of my own military background, as well as my childhood in Texas during the 50s and 60s, to establish the social, cultural, and geographic setting, as well as trying to make the language used by the characters as credible as possible. None of the specific incidents in the stories are real, but they're all based on historical events of the era after the Civil War when America was opening up the western frontier to settlement and development.

I do research on a continuing basis seeking new story ideas, and to make sure that the equipment, tactics, and events have a ring of credibility. For instance, during my research, I discovered that the US Cavalrymen, contrary to what you might see in the movies, didn't use repeating rifles during this period. They used the single shot Springfield because the army viewed it as more reliable and durable than the new Winchester repeaters, and it was cheaper. Even in those days, the government was concerned about the bottom line. I also learned that white soldiers received $24 dollars a month pay, and black soldiers

$12 – which wasn't bad money in the 1870s when you consider that when I enlisted in 1962, my pay was $72 per month.

So, you see, ideas for your writing can come from anywhere. You just have to open all the doors and windows in your mind and let the light shine in.

Where Ideas Come From – Part 2

This one was published on May 6, 2015

When I started writing the Al Pennyback mystery series, I didn't have a specific sub-genre in mind. It's not a hardboiled mystery with a hero who is always battling bad guys; nor is it a procedural mystery – I go light on the technical aspects of crimes, criminals, or police procedures. I was just going for a good story that had a crime as a central element, which the hero, Al Pennyback, would then set about solving.

My main motivation for writing this particular series was the fact that I live in the Washington, DC area, and have for more than 30 years, and most of the stories set in this locale are about politicians, spies, or high-powered lobbyists. I know that the average Joe and Jane who happens to call the Washington metro area home lives a life that can be just as exciting as the K Street crowd, or the boys across the river in McLean, so, about ten years ago I started drafting.

My first, *Color Me Dead*, went through more than six years of rewriting; the title changed, the central plot changed, and most importantly, the name and background of the main character changed. I no longer remember what I called him at first, but, one day as I was sweating over the tenth or twentieth draft, Al Pennyback was born. He's an African-American; after all, the area is predominantly African-American; he's retired military; being retired military, I can relate to that, and the area also has loads of retired military people; and he's a sucker for puzzles and unsolved mysteries. Despite, or because of, his military background, he hates guns, preferring to use his wits or his martial arts ability to get out of tight spots. He's a widower; gives him an air of sympathy; but, has a girlfriend. The sex scenes are only hinted at. I think too many modern mysteries go overboard on the sex. And, the language is mostly mild. On occasion, Al or one of the characters lets fly with an earthy expletive, because that's the way people talk after all, but you won't find curse words on every page.

That's sort of the definition of a cozy mystery; cosy in British English; but, I didn't set out to write cozies. Despite that, one of my British readers has decided that's the sub-genre of at least one of the stories in the series, *Dead Man's Cove*. He gave it such a good review, I don't have the heart to argue the point.

Following the advice given in most books on writing, I try to show, not tell. I let the characters' dialogue and action move the story rather than filling page after page with exposition or descriptions.

Now, the question one might well ask is; where do the ideas for this series come from? The answer is – everywhere. I read newspapers, print and online, and every edition has at least one story idea. *Till Death Do Us Part*, for instance, came from an article I read in a South African newspaper on a flight from Capetown to Copenhagen a few years ago about a couple who'd come to Johannesburg on vacation and been victims of a carjacking. The wife was killed, but the husband escaped unharmed. It turned out later that he'd arranged the incident in order to get rid of his wife. I changed the setting to Jamaica and was off to the races.

I've done two books about radical militias, *Dead, White, and Blue* and *Deadly Intentions*. The proliferation of militias and other hate groups in the U.S. over the past several decades has always concerned me, so this was a natural.

Deadline started out as a story about scams against lonely women, but about one-third into the first draft I decided to throw a ghost in just for the heck of it. I'm a bit agnostic about ghosts – I don't know that they are real, but I don't know that they're not, so there you are.

Whatever motivates the story idea, my main objective is to write a story that keeps the reader wanting to turn the page to see what happens next.

There you have it; that's where story ideas come from. I'll bet if you stop and think about it, you'll find that your inspiration is similar.

How to Handle Dialogue

If you're writing fiction, you'll have characters who must interact with each other through dialogue. Sounds easy, but it's not as easy as you think. You see, you might be tempted to have your characters speak just like people do in real life. Before you do that, read the following.

Writing dialogue isn't easy, but well-written dialogue can help to move your story along. Following are a few hints for writing effective dialogue.

Writers' guides advise starting stories with action as soon as possible. 'Plunge your reader right into the middle of the action,' most urge—except those on writing the profound piece of literary fiction, which are often as hard to understand as the works they're designed to teach you to write. Anyway, that's not what we're about here. Here, I want to talk to you about writing good stories; the 'once upon a time' types that have entertained us for generations. So, how do you 'plunge your reader into the middle of the action?' Well, having your characters tell the story through their dialogue is a good way to start. Dialogue can help get action going, be used to vary the pace of a story, or to build suspense.

Opening a story with a character saying something is almost guaranteed to make a reader want to know what happens next. Provided that what's said is related to the plot, *and* that you've done an effective job of writing that dialogue.

Effective dialogue can be used to advance a story, foreshadow events, provide backstory without having to resort to flashbacks (which disrupt the flow of a story), provide historical or technical information, or drop hints or clues. Dialogue can flesh out your character and help avoid pages of boring narrative exposition which most people skip over anyway. The key is to make your dialogue realistic without being boring. Get dialogue wrong, and most readers will drop your book like a hot donut.

The following tips will help you write dialogue that will achieve your aim of writing stories that readers keep coming back to.

Learn to listen: If you want to write realistic dialogue, you have to be a good listener. On the subway, in the store, or at parties, pay attention to the way people talk. Make note of the words they use, unusual speech patterns or pronunciations, and their body language when they speak.

Write it the way it should be said, not the way it actually is: One thing you'll learn from eavesdropping on (listening to) people is that they can often be quite boring when they speak. Incomplete sentences, verbal pauses, mispronounced words, mangled grammar—I could go on and on—is how most people *really* talk. If you have a character who does this, be careful not to have every bit of dialogue like that. Show it sparingly, just to establish the habit, maybe a bit more in the beginning and then just a drop here and there afterwards. Readers will remember. The same thing with dialect, whether regional or national; don't overdo it. Your dialogue should read *like* a conversation, but not be a duplication of an actual verbal exchange. Edit out unnecessary verbal pauses (except for those needed to establish a character's identity), and anything else that doesn't advance your story or identify your character. As Alfred Hitchcock said, "a good story is life, with the dull parts taken out."

Speech tags: Speech tags are a good way to identify who is talking. You'll often see things like 'he enthused,' or 'he shouted angrily.' My best advice is to avoid such tags, or keep them to the barest minimum. No, strike that—don't use them. The old standby 'said,' and occasionally 'asked,' should be used instead, and even they should be used sparingly. You should really avoid tags like 'growled,' 'spit,' and the like Here are two examples of dialogue.

Version one

"Don't touch me," Angela said angrily.
"Why not?" John asked dejectedly.

"Because, I don't love you," she said sadly.

Version two

Angela pulled away as John reached for her. "Don't touch me," she said. Her eyes blazed as she looked up at him. "W-why not," John said. He had the look of a kid who didn't get the bike he wanted for Christmas.
"Because . . . I don't . . . love you." Angela turned away so he wouldn't see the tears that were beginning to flow down her cheeks.

Do you see the difference? Which do you think is more effective?

Have a good mix of dialogue and action: Just as page upon page of exposition can be boring, a long stretch of dialogue uninterrupted by any narrative to put it into perspective can be jarring. Some writing coaches suggest some kind of action, or beat, after every three lines of dialogue. I don't like one-size-fits-all rules, so I tend to put in action whenever I feel the characters have talked long enough and the reader needs to have other senses engaged to stay in the story. Putting character actions in with speech helps the reader to get a better sense of the reality of the scene and helps to break up the page. Note in the dialogue example above how action was used to show character emotion.

Be careful with language stereotypes, slang, and profanity:
In real life, people speak using regional or national dialects,
use slang, and some even curse like sailors. In order to
clearly identify characters and establish credibility, some of
this might be necessary in your fiction. Just be careful not to
overdo it. The days when Stephen Foster's parody of black
speech in his tales of Br'er Rabbit and Br'er Fox are over, and
not just because it's politically incorrect—it's just wrong and
unnecessary. If you have a character with a strong regional
speech pattern, establish it when the character's first
introduced with just the amount required to fix it in a
reader's mind, and from then on, use mainly standard
English. The same advice applies to slang and profanity. In
a short story I wrote and published online several years ago,
I had a character travel from Detroit to East Texas. I've
visited the former and grew up in the latter, so I had the
characters use the speech patterns I remembered. A reader
living in the East Texas area thought my Detroit speech
patterns were perfect, but was offended at what she thought
was a demeaning portrayal of the slow twangy speech of East
Texas. The fact is, both were correct, but I'd overdone it, but
using it in every bit of dialogue, rather than just establishing
that this is how the people in each locale talked and then
switch to standard English. From that I learned my lesson, or
lairn't muh lessen, as the folks back home in East Texas
would say when they talked about how to use seasoning in
cooking; use just enough to give it flavor.

Don't have your characters making speeches: I don't like rules, but here's one that I think is useful. You shouldn't have a single character's dialogue be more than a quarter page without a break—action, or another character speaking. Dialogue is a good way to introduce information, but do not have your character recite the Encyclopedia Americana for five pages. It's best to have information come out in bits here and pieces there, just as it does in real life. Unless a character is making a speech (which should also be broken up with action, or summarized in narrative) it is unrealistic to think that he or she would be able to speak for a long time without being interrupted. Doesn't happen in real life, and it shouldn't happen in your fiction.

What goes on behind the Bedroom Door?

This was my very first blog post for Alex Cavanaugh's *Insecure Writer's Support Group* published on October 2, 2013. In it I tackled what I believe might just be one of the toughest nuts for a writer to crack.

I got the idea for this post from Jacqui Murray's posting on writing about love. Jacqui Murray is a fellow writer and blogger whose posts I particularly like. The hang-up for me is writing about the physical manifestation of love, or to put it mildly, sex. This is a problem, really, because I do a mystery series about an unmarried private detective who has a live-in girlfriend, who also happens to be relatively attractive to the opposite sex.

There are, therefore, times and scenes when sex would be appropriate, but whenever I come to one of those points in a story, my fingers seem to freeze. I'm not a prude, I'll have you know. But, I do have some regular readers who I know would be shocked, and perhaps even offended, if my finger should slip and I became too graphic.

I've wrestled with this problem over 17 books in the series; on occasion straying a bit into the slightly detailed description of the act, sometimes just alluding to it with euphemistic language, and sometimes having an entire story without one amorous encounter.

After a long time of experimenting, I've finally hit on a way to handle the delicate aspects of relations between characters in my stories; one that I hope works. Firstly, I don't include a sex scene in a story unless it is germane to the particular story; either to show the developing relationship between characters, or is somehow related to the events of the story. An example of the last is, a character's motive for murder might be that the victim once sexually assaulted, jilted, or cheated on her.

Once I've decided that sex should be a part of the story, the next challenge is how to handle it. Unless you're writing a romance or porn novel, a blow-by-blow description is, in my view, inappropriate. I find, rather, that a description of the actions characters take in the early stage of a seduction (conversation, eye contact, etc.) sets the scene, and when the characters finally head for the bedroom, like the old movies from the 1950s, you can fade the scene out – most readers will know what's coming next. This has the added benefit of allowing readers to use their imaginations, which is a plus for your writing.

This way of handling physical relations might not work for everyone. I have to confess that I'm of a generation that grew up in a more inhibited era than kids of today, so my way is comfortable for me. If you happen to be the bodice-ripping, bosom-heaving type who loves to write long, steamy encounters that are the mainstay of romance novels, more power to you.

As for me, excuse me while I turn out the lights. I'll see you in the morning. (Lap dissolve to crashing waves, then fade to black)

Which is More Important; Plot or Character?

A debate that has raged forever is that about which is more important in fiction, plot or character. Which contributes to a good story? I can imagine that when the first ancient storyteller stood before his tribe, someone was asking, which is more important, the theme of the story, or the characters in it.

Every writer, or wannabe writer, has an opinion on the issue, as do the legions of critics and commentators.

Some say that a good plot is essential to the success of a story, while others doggedly maintain that the important thing in a good story is the development and growth of the characters—especially the main protagonist.

While I write mainly westerns and mysteries, genres which must be carefully plotted in order to be successful, I have to confess that I tend toward the view that, no matter how compelling the plot, if I feel nothing for the characters, the story won't hold my interest. I firmly believe in the words of **author Christopher LaFarge, who in an essay, 'Some personal beliefs,' in the 1965 edition of *The Writer's Book*, said;** "However well plotted and constructed the story, however solid or tenuous its intentions, however admirable its purpose, it is nothing at all unless the characters within it have a good measure of reality." In order for characters to be accepted by readers, LaFarge wrote, no matter how weird they may be, they must have 'universal qualities,' even if those qualities be unadmirable.

You have to make readers care about your characters: This is advice I follow in everything I write. While I plot carefully—well, somewhat carefully—in long and short pieces, the mainstay of each story I write are the characters that inhabit the world I've created. Sometimes the plots are not as strong as they perhaps they should be, but when I get the characters right, the stories work. I'll give you an example. Years ago, I wrote a story, 'Dead Letter,' about a loser, Louis Dumkowski, who, unable to pay a debt owed to a loan shark, attempted to hide by moving. In a twist on the traditional stories of inefficient bureaucracy, the Post Office tracked him down to deliver a threatening letter from the loan shark. The plot wasn't very complicated, and I spent a good bit of the story describing Louis, and the last ten percent describing his assailant shooting him through the door with a shotgun. I posted it on an online short story site, and promptly forgot about it. It had just been an exercise in writing a story using a given first sentence prompt, and like I said, the plot was really simplistic. So, you can imagine my surprise when I checked back on the site and found that it had been among the most read stories, and had garnered a number of comments. Two, in particular, struck me:

"I enjoyed the tension you created and wished the story had been longer. We barely get to know Louis, and then Vinnie kills him! Could you pick up Vinnie's story? Or, maybe Louis can survive the assault?"
"I think it would be interesting to read on if Louis survived and the story continued. In this short piece, we know enough about Louis to want to know more."

There were others that talked about the character as well. Other than the sense of suspense that was built up, mainly through describing Louis through talking about the mess he'd gotten himself into, no one talked about the plot or theme of the story. It was all about the character, and how they felt they'd come to know and care about him. I've had the same reaction to my novels. I've even had a couple of readers contact me and tell me that they've fallen love with Al Pennyback, the protagonist in my mystery novels—including one fan who thought the plot of the particular book stank and chided me, because dear Al deserved better. My point in all this: make readers care about your characters and they'll come back for more.

You Got Your Book Written. What's Next?

Well, here we are. You've kicked the insecurity habit, chained yourself to your chair and, writing 1,000 to 2,000 words a day, and finally got that book written. You put it aside a few days to let it cool off, and then spent another week or so going over it mercilessly, editing and polishing—oh, did I forget to say, writing, especially fiction, is really about re-writing—and you're convinced the hardest part is behind you. Sorry, my friend, but the hardest part is yet to come.

First, you have to get it published, and that can be a real kick in the pants. You have two rational choices. You can start sending it out to traditional publishers, waiting for the inevitable rejection slips, and sending it out again; or, you can take the route that many authors are taking these days, and independently publish it. I decided long ago, for reasons quite personal to me, to go the independent route. The whole indie vs. traditional argument is a subject for a whole other book, so I won't go into it here. You have to make the decision that's right for you. I will, however, offer a word of caution. You're likely to see any number of ads and solicitations from outfits offering to publish your book—for a fee. Often it's quite a sizeable investment. If you chose to go that way, it's your choice, but I personally advise against it. Also, watch out for companies that don't charge, but offer no advance, offer no editing services, over price your book making it uncompetitive, and lock you into a long contract giving you no rights to your book.

Now, I have that off my chest. Let's talk about the next big hurdle you as an author will face; promoting your book. You'll have to do this whether you go indie or traditional, so pay attention. My advice, for obvious reasons though, will be from the perspective of an indie author, so if you do go the traditional route and are lucky enough to find a publisher, some of this stuff won't apply. I trust, though, that you're smart enough to discern the differences, so let's get down to business.

Marketing Your Book is Like a Trip to the Dentist

This is was second posting for Alex Cavanaugh's *Insecure Writer's Support Group* posted on November 6, 2013 Here I addressed the bete noire of many writers; marketing your work after it's completed.

Make no mistake about it, writing; serious writing; is hard work. After deciding *what* to write, you struggle with *how* to most effectively express it in words, sentences, and paragraphs. When you plotted, planned, and shaped those words, you then have to face the daunting task of re-writing and editing to make sure you've expressed yourself in the best possible way.

If you think, after you've done all that, the job is done; stop, have a cup of coffee and listen up. The job's just started. Unless you're writing merely for your personal amusement, you want to be read, and that means you have to take the next step – and, it's a big one. You have to get what you've written in front of readers, and hopefully keep it there long enough for them to read and enjoy it.

That's right; I'm talking about the m-word. Like trips to the dentist, marketing your writing is unpleasant and uncomfortable, but ultimately necessary if you're

to succeed in this line of work we call writing. There's that 'work' word again.

There are a number of ways to market your books. Social media, public engagements, ads, are all ways to get your efforts in front of an audience and, hopefully, create a buzz about it that leads to more readers and more sales.

One method that has generated a lot of comment and controversy of late is using give-aways as a means of promoting your writing. Some writers swear by it, while others swear at it, and vehemently avoid it. After all, the second group maintains, if your work is free it will be seen as having no value.

Before enlisting in this group, though, I recommend you think about it for a while. It might seem counter-intuitive, but offering people something for free can be a way to get them to buy. Big stores do it, and successfully. My own experience with this form of marketing offers a look at some of the advantages of this method.

Like many, I was reluctant at first. My thought was; I've worked long and hard on this book, why should I

just give it away? But, I'm always up for trying
something new, so I decided to give it a go.

Most of my books are available on Amazon in Kindle
version, and the Kindle Direct Publishing (KDP)
program enables an author who enrolls a book to offer
it free for a designated period, provided it is exclusive
to the program during the free period. You can get the
details of the program at https://kdp.amazon.com/,
but here's how it's worked for me.

I do two series; a western/historical fiction series
about the Buffalo Soldiers, and a mystery series. I
dipped my feet in the water by offering a couple of my
mysteries free for the five-day period. Each time, there
were hundreds of downloads (primarily in the US
market, with a few in the UK). There were no big
upticks in sales, but I did notice that whenever I
offered one book in the series free, there were modest
sales of all the other titles. I then decided to try it with
the Buffalo Soldier series, which were just beginning to
catch on. The first couple of times, sales went up
moderately each time for each book in the series, but
nothing to write home about.

Then, in May 2013, I released the fifth book in the
series, *Buffalo Soldier: Renegade.* After two weeks of
lackluster sales, I decided to try a free promotion.
During the five-day promotion, there were nearly 400
downloads, mainly in the US market, but it was the

two week period following the promotion that opened my eyes. In addition to another 400 sales of that title, readers purchased 5 to 10 copies per week of each of the other titles. My royalty revenue for that month was over $800, which isn't a bad return for a loss leader.

That wasn't the end of it, either. The next book in the series, *Buffalo Soldier: Escort Duty* was released in September. I waited a week and then offered it free. There were 336 downloads during a short three-day period, and then the week after it ended, sales of that title were approaching the 200 mark, and again, 5 to 10 copies per week of each of the five preceding titles. Revenue thus far is nearing the $500 mark, and it has even generated sales of the paperback versions of each.

Maybe offering free books is not for everyone, but I'm sold on this as an effective marketing tool. It's not the only one, and if you don't have a large number of books on your backlist, it might not be worth the effort. But, it certainly shouldn't be ignored. It hasn't hurt the value of my books. I continue to get fairly decent reviews on Amazon, and repeat readers who are willing to shell out money to read them, so until I experience a drop in sales I will continue to do what entrepreneurs in other sectors do, and do quite successfully.

How to Promote Your Book for Free

I wrote this for Alec Cavanaugh's *Insecure Writers Support Group* on September 2, 2015.

I want to address an issue that I know concerns everyone who writes for publication; book promotion, and how to avoid some of the schemes floating around, and at the same time, promote your book without having to shell out a lot of money.

Book promotion is like going to the dentist. It's one of those things that is unpleasant, but necessary for good health, or in the case of a book, getting sales. Social media, as pervasive as it is these days, is a good way to promote your published work, or even create buzz for a work in progress, but the problem is knowing how to use it.

I've found Twitter to be a highly effective means to get word out about my books. So, apparently, have thousands—if not millions—of other people. As with any technique that works, it has also spawned a whole new industry of people who offer, for a fee, to help you get your word out to the Twitterverse.

I'm not calling these offers scams, because the majority of them are probably honest offers. But, honest or not, they are unnecessary. Why pay $50 upwards to have tweets posted about your book by someone else, when you could, with a little effort, probably do the same thing yourself? Or, you could find one of the free retweet services, such as CoPromote, to do it. I've been using this one for several months now, and during time have reached over 4 million new potential readers, and seen a 25% increase in monthly book sales, both paperback and e-Book. CoPromote is a relatively easy concept. You sign up, link your account to your Twitter, Tumblr, and YouTube accounts. You then pick a Twitter, Tumblr or YouTube post to promote and highlight it (the instructions are easy). After you've selected a post to promote, you scroll through posts by other members and select up to ten per day. The posts you select are promoted on your accounts, and other members promote your post. My average number of shares during the two week promotion period has been 150,000 to just over 300,000 new shares. That's a lot of new readers. When I first signed up, Facebook posts could also be linked, but due to technical problems, this is no longer possible. The web masters at CoPromote say they're working on the problem, so we'll just have to wait and see what happens. There is, though, a way around the problem. I have my Facebook and Twitter accounts linked, so that when I tweet, it also does a Facebook post. Helps others more than me, other than the fact that it helps enhance my reputation as someone who promotes others--not a bad thing for a writer.

I use CoPromote primarily to promote published books, but have also used it for other projects, such as my photography. This gives me extended reach to new readers without having to do frequent sales pitches on my own accounts. And, it costs me nothing. Now, you can't get better advertising than that. I'd be interested in hearing from anyone else who has had experience with CoPromote or any other free book promotion site.

Overcome Your Fear of Public Speaking and Sell More Books

Most people have an almost irrational fear of speaking before an audience – many fear that more than death. But, for a way to get your writing known by a wider audience, using public speaking opportunities is one that should not be ignored.

I have, like many, had a fear of making public speeches. When I was a teenager, during my freshman year in high school, I would get tongue-tied and absolutely panicky at the prospect of getting up in front of a group and talking. Luckily, I had a freshman home room teacher who recognized the fear and had a way to help me overcome it. During the early weeks of the semester, she would make me stand in front of the classroom until I said something – anything. Her shock therapy worked. After a few weeks, I found it possible to speak without stuttering, and after I said something funny one morning and cracked the whole room up, my fear was mostly conquered. I'm now a regular on the podium, speaking on a range of topics with which I'm familiar. I still get the occasional attack of nerves, but once I start interacting with an audience, the jitters disappear.

Enough background – what you want to know is how I use these occasions to promote my books. It's really simple, and it has worked well for me.

First, I always take a good supply of my business cards to events. My cards contain links to my blogs and to my Amazon author page which contains 'buy' links for all my books. I also take along a few copies of books – preferably, but not always, related to the subject of my speech. I place them where they can be easily seen by the audience, and during breaks and at the conclusion of my remarks, I'm always asked about them by two or three attendees. As we discuss them, I hand out cards. After each such event, I've noticed an uptick in my sales – and, not just the books on display, but others as well. After one speech on ethics at the Army Command and General Staff College, for instance, where I had copies of my Buffalo Soldier western/historical series (appropriate to the venue since the Buffalo Soldier memorial is there), sales of one of the books in the series jumped to 800 for the month, and each other volume in the series had increases from 2 – 3 copies to over 20 each. In addition, the staff college foundation magazine did a feature on me and my books, which still generates sales of that series.

At a speaking engagement at Chautauqua Institution in upstate New York, I got into a conversation on writing during a break in the session, and several people asked for my card or for links to my books online. Again, that month I had an uptick in sales.

Contrary to some cynics, word of mouth *is* an effective way to sell books, and one of the most effective mouths to start that process rolling is your own. Public speaking shouldn't be scary. When you stand before an audience – hopefully, talking about a subject with which you're familiar – you can and should be in control of the situation. Like any other skill, it improves with practice. So, get over that fear of public speaking, and get out there and sell your books!

A Final Word, and a Little Bit About the Author

There you have it; the methods I used (well a good percentage of them) to overcome the insecurity that was preventing me from writing. Here, I want to tell you a little about myself, beyond the writing.

I mentioned in the introduction that I've been writing fiction since my teens. I'd been making up stories, though, for as long as I can remember. Ever since I read an Edgar Rice Burroughs' book in fourth grade, I'd been hooked on it. When I was twelve or thirteen, my home room teacher suggested I write a story and submit it to a short story competition that was sponsored by the Sunday school magazine they gave out in church each week. I figured, what the heck, and spent a few days coming up with a story about a boy who witnessed the Last Supper or something like that, and sent it off. I promptly forgot about it—at that age, most boys have the attention span of a fruit fly—until two months later I got a letter with a check inside. My story had won first place and I received the princely sum of ten dollars. What hooked me, though, was that a few months later, when the magazine was passed out in church, there was my story, with my name underneath. I was hooked.

After graduating from high school and joining the army, I dabbled in writing for a few years. I was a regular contributor to the Pup Tent Poets section of the European edition of *Stars and Stripes*, an English-language publication for GIs and their families serving overseas, and even got the occasional small article published.

Fast forward ten years, and I'd gone from buck private to captain, and was the assistant public affairs officer for all of Ft. Bragg, NC, responsible for command information programs at the largest army base in the world. I was also the equivalent of executive editor of the *Paraglide*, the base paper with a circulation of over 100,000, making it the third or fourth largest circulation newspaper in North Carolina. I did articles, photo layouts, and art work for the paper (in addition to writing, I'm also an avid photographer, cartoonist, and graphic artist, which came to the attention of editors of other papers in the area. Pretty soon, I was doing articles and theatrical reviews for the Fayetteville, NC newspaper, photographic support for the Fayetteville Arts Council, and was the editorial cartoonist for a weekly newspaper in Spring Lake, NC. At the same time, I was doing articles, photography, and artwork for magazines around the country, including *Ebony, Essence,* and a few others that are no longer being published.

You'll notice the little cartoons scattered about this book, some relating to the subject matter, some apparently not. I'm a doodler by nature. I'm always making little drawings in the margins of notebooks or on any flat surface. These are just my doodles to relieve the monotony of huge blocks of text. Hope you like them.

Moreover, I hope you've liked this book, and at the risk of boring repetition, I hope you'll find a nugget or two of wisdom within its pages.

As Porky Pig always said at the end of the Saturday morning cartoons, "T-that's all f-folks!" Happy writing.

"Now, while you're busy writing your book, I'm off for some much needed vacation."

Bibliography and References

The following are books and other items in my personal writing reference library. They are listed in no particular order, but in the order that I think of or use them. You'll notice that some of them are quite old, but I hope you'll find them as useful as I have.

General Reference

Webster's New Universal Unabridged Dictionary. New World Dictionaries, Cleveland, OH. 1983.

The MacMillan Dictionary of Quotations, Chartwell Books, Edison, NJ. 2000.

Perrin, Porter G. and Wilma R. Ebbitt, *Writer's Guide and Index to English, 5th edition.* Scott, Foresman and Company, Glenview, IL. 1972.

Browne, Renni and Dave King, *Self-Editing for Fiction Writers,* William Morrow, New York. 2004.

Barr, Chris, ed., *The Yahoo! Style Guide,* St. Martin's

Griffin, New York. 2010.

Hood, Ann, *Creating Character Emotions,* Story Press, Cincinnati, OH. 1998.

Bell, James Scott, *Plot & Structure,* Writer's Digest Books, Cincinnati, OH. 2004.

Bell, James Scott, *Revision & Self-Editing,* Writers' Digest Books, Cincinnati, OH. 2008.

Kempton, Gloria, *Dialogue: Techniques and exercises for crafting effective dialogue,* Writer's Digest Books, Cincinnati, OH. 2004.

Kress, Nancy, *Characters, Emotion & Viewpoint,* Writer's Digest Books, Cincinnati, OH. 2005.

Rozelle, Ron, *Description & Setting,* Writer's Digest Books, Cincinnati, OH. 2005.

King, Stephen, *On Writing: A Memoir of the Craft,* Scribner, New York. 2000.

Baty, Chris, *No Plot? No Problem!: A Low-stress, High-velocity Guide to Writing a Novel in 30 Days,* Chronical Books, San Francisco. 2004.

Mystery Writing

Roth, Martin, *The Writer's Complete Crime Reference Book.* Writer's Digest Books, Cincinnati, OH. 1993.

Glanze, Walter D., et al, *The Mosby Medical Encyclopedia,* Penguin Group, New York. 1992.

McAleer, John and Andrew McAleer, *Mystery Writing in*

a *Nutshell,* James A. Rock and Co., Rockville, MD. 2007.

Riviere, Bill, *The Gunner's Bible,* Doubleday and Company, New York. 1965.

Newton, Michael, *Armed and Dangerous: A Writer's Guide to Weapons,* Writer's Digest Books, Cincinnati, OH. 1990.

Stevens, Serita Deborah with Anne Klarner, *Deadly Doses: A Writers' Guide to Poisons,* Writer's Digest Books, Cincinnati, OH. 1990.

Blythe, Hal et al, *Private Eyes: A Writer's Guide to Private Investigators,* Writers' Digest Books, Cincinnati, OH. 1993.

Wingate, Anne, *Scene of the Crime: A Writer's Guide to Crime-Scene Investigations,* Writer's Digest Books, Cincinnati, OH. 1992.

Bintliff, Russell, *Police Procedural: A Writer's Guide to the Police and How they Work,* Writers' Digest Books, Cincinnati, OH. 1993.

Wilson, Keith D., *Cause of Death: A Writer's Guide to Death, Murder, & Forensic Medicine,* Writer's Digest Books, Cincinnati, OH. 1992.

Norville, Barbara, *Writing the Modern Mystery,* Writer's Digest Books, Cincinnati, OH. 1986.

Treat, Lawrence, ed., *Mystery Writer's Handbook,* Writer's Digest, Cincinnati, OH. 1976.

Westerns and Historical Writing

Adams, Ramon F., *Western Words: A Dictionary of the Old West,* Hippocrene Books, New York. 1998.

Morton, Nik, *Write a Western in 30 Days,* Compass Books, Winchester, UK. 2013.

Cooper, Jeff, *Guns of the Old West,* Paladin Press, Boulder, CO. 2008.

Vogel, Colin, *The Complete Horse Care Manual,* DK Publishing, NYC. 1995.

Foster-Harris, William, *The Look of the Old West,* Skyhorse Publishing, New York. 2007.

Marston, Doris Ricker, *A Guide to Writing History,* Writer's Digest, Cincinnati, OH. 1976.

Other Genres

Bova, Ben with Anthony R. Lewis, *Space Travel: A writer's guide to the science of interplanetary and interstellar travel,* Writer's Digest Books, Cincinnati, OH. 1997.